The Amazing Dandelion

MILLICENT E. SELSAM
AND JEROME WEXLER

William Morrow and Company
New York 1977

LIBRARY OF CONGRESS CATALOGING IN PUBLICATION DATA

Selsam, Millicent Ellis, 1912-
    The amazing dandelion.

    Summary: Discusses the life cycle of the dandelion, an extremely hearty
plant with often overlooked nutritional value.
    1. Dandelions–Juvenile literature. [1. Dandelions]
I. Wexler, Jerome. II. Title.
QK495.C74S35   583'.55   77-9029
ISBN 0-688-22129-7
ISBN 0-688-32129-1 lib. bdg.

The author and photographer thank
Dr. Howard S. Irwin,
President of the New York Botanical Gardens,
for checking the text and photographs of this book.

ACKNOWLEDGMENTS FOR PHOTOGRAPHS

Lynwood Chace, National Audubon Society, 30
Constance Porter, National Audubon Society, 32
United States Department of Agriculture, 44

BY THE SAME AUTHOR

To Priscilla

The dandelion is a most successful plant.
One year a single plant may grow in a field.

6   A few years later
    the field may be covered with dandelions!

How do they spread so quickly?
You can find out
if you follow the life story of the dandelion.

A dandelion seed is sprouting.

Soon you see a young dandelion plant
called a "seedling."
It doesn't look much like our familiar dandelion yet.

10   Later in the season
the leaves are spread out in a circle,
or rosette.
The leaves have jagged "teeth."
So people in France called the plant "*dent-de-lion*,"
which means "lion's tooth."
The dandelion was brought to America from Europe,
and after a while
dent-de-lion came to be known as dandelion.
The scientific name of the dandelion is
Taraxacum officinale
(Ta-*rax*-ah-cuhm o-fiss-i-*nah*-lay).

Under the ground
there is a central long, thick tap root
with side branches coming out from it.

12   A flower stem rises from the center
of the rosette of leaves.
There may be one, two, or several flower stalks.

The stalks are hollow.
A white, sticky sap oozes out
from the cut end of this stalk.
At one time scientists tried
to make rubber out of this sticky sap,
but they were not too successful.
However, there is a Russian dandelion
known as *kok-saghyz*
that does yield rubber.

The flower bud opens.

The "flower" is not a single flower
but a cluster of many of them
packed closely together like a bouquet.
Sometime try to count the flowers.
There should be between 150 and 200 of them.

DAISY

THISTLE

The daisy, thistle, and lettuce
belong in the same plant family as the dandelion.
All members of this family are called "composites,"
and their "flowers" are really clusters
of many small flowers growing together.

LETTUCE

18   The picture on the left shows
a single dandelion flower about to open.
The ovary, where the seed will develop,
is at the bottom.
Above it is a circle of fine, silky hairs
called a "pappus."
The rest of the flower has not yet opened.

The flower on the right is opening.
The single petal moves away from the central tube.
The tube is made up of five anthers
(sacs of pollen) joined together.

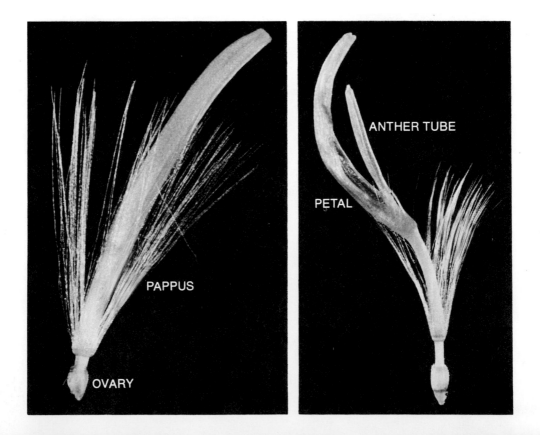

Out of the anther tube
a part called the "style" emerges.
It is connected to the ovary
at the bottom of the flower.
Its fuzzy sides act like a brush
and bring the pollen out from the tube of anthers.

The tip of the style, which is called the "stigma,"
begins to separate.

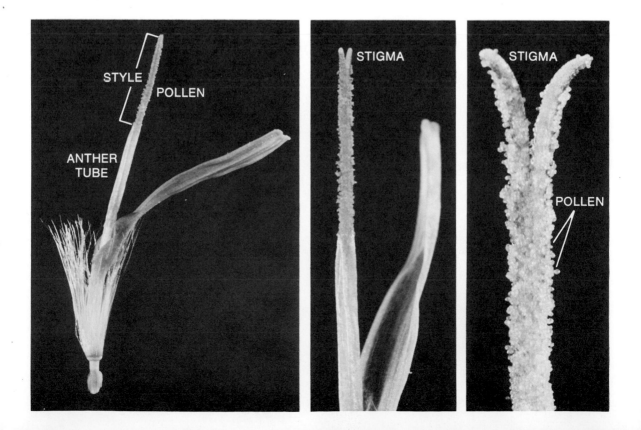

20 Bees, wasps, flies, butterflies, and beetles
come to suck the nectar
in the bottom of the dandelion flowers.
In so doing, they carry the pollen from flower to flower.
The bodies of many of these insects
are covered with short, stiff hairs.
The hairs pick up pollen
as the insect moves through the flower head.
The stigma tips are sticky.
When an insect loaded with pollen brushes against them,
some of the pollen sticks to the stigmas.
In this way pollination is completed.

If by chance a flower is not pollinated by insects,
the dandelion flower can pollinate itself.
The stigma makes a complete loop,
and its inner receptive surface comes in contact
with the pollen on the outside of the anther tube.

22   In addition, dandelion flowers can form seeds
      that grow into new plants
      without any pollination at all.
      In fact, scientists believe that most dandelion seeds
      are formed in this way.

If the flowers are pollinated,
the pollen grains send out tubes
that grow down the style to the ovary.
Inside each ovary is a single ovule.
The contents of one pollen tube
join with the contents of the ovule.
This joining of the pollen grain with the ovule
is called "fertilization."
The ovule now becomes a seed.
The ovary around it becomes a dry one-seeded fruit
called an "achene" (*a*-keen).
(Any part of the plant that contains a seed or seeds
is technically a fruit.)
So what people often say are dandelion seeds
are really fruits with one seed inside.

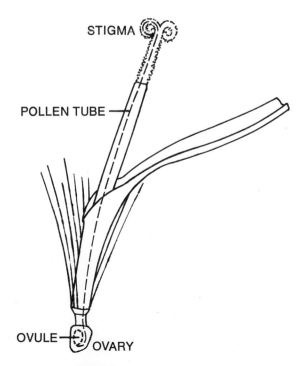

STIGMA

POLLEN TUBE

OVULE — OVARY

24 Dandelion flowers open at eight in the morning and close about three in the afternoon every day. But after pollination, the flower parts shrivel and the flower closes up for one to two weeks.

Then something new happens inside the flower head.
The pappuses grow taller.
The dried-up remains of the flowers sit on top of them.
Soon they fall off the seed head.

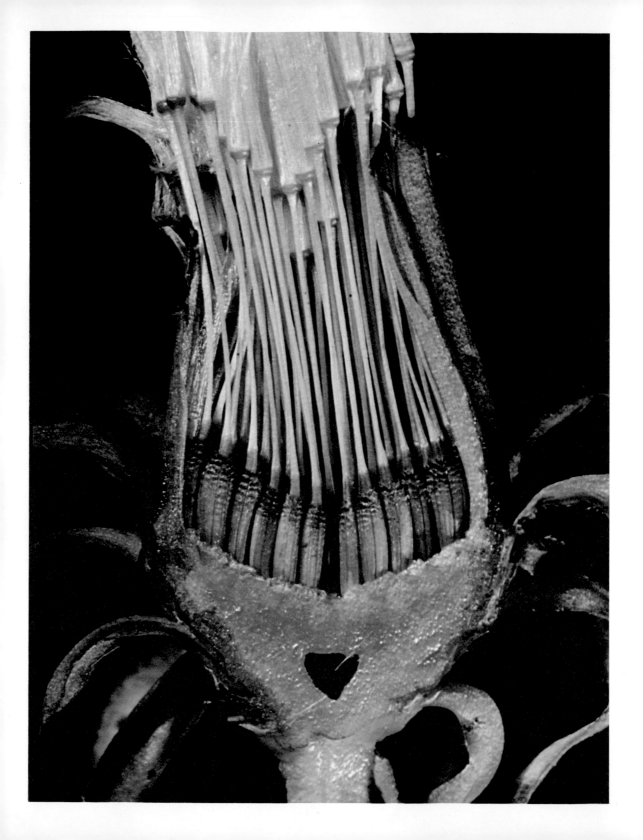

On the left is a cross section of the seed head.
You can see the brown achenes at the bottom.

The seed head begins to open.

The slightest breeze will send
the silky gray parachutes into the air.
At the bottom they carry the achenes,
each with its single seed.

32 Some may fall on rocks where they cannot grow.
Some may fly into a bird's nest where they cannot grow.
Some may even fly into the ears of the cows
grazing on the grass,
but they cannot grow there either.
Some may fall into streams and rivers
and be carried to sea where they cannot grow.
But there are so many seeds in the air
that though a lot of them are lost,
some seeds are sure to find their way into soil
where they *can* grow.

Usually the pappus falls off
when the achene hits the ground.
The achene has hooks on it
that help keep it attached to the soil.

But sometimes the pappus stays on,
and the next wind lifts it into the air again.
Dandelion fruits keep flying.
A light wind carries them
about a quarter of a block.
Gale winds can carry them twenty-five miles.

The dandelion is a never-say-die plant
in that it has so many ways of surviving
under difficult circumstances.

34 The fruits with their parachutes
    are able to close up in wet weather
    and open wide when the air is dry.
    This adaptation enables the seeds
    to be carried far from the mother plant.

    Try this experiment.
    Put several stalks of dandelions with fluffy seed heads
    in each of two glasses of water.
    Cover one with a jar that fits over it snugly.
    Leave the other open to the air.
    Put both in sunlight
    and let them stand for at least twenty-four hours.
    The parachute hairs fold together
    in the covered glass where the air is moist.

    These three photographs show
    how the pappus opens in dry air.

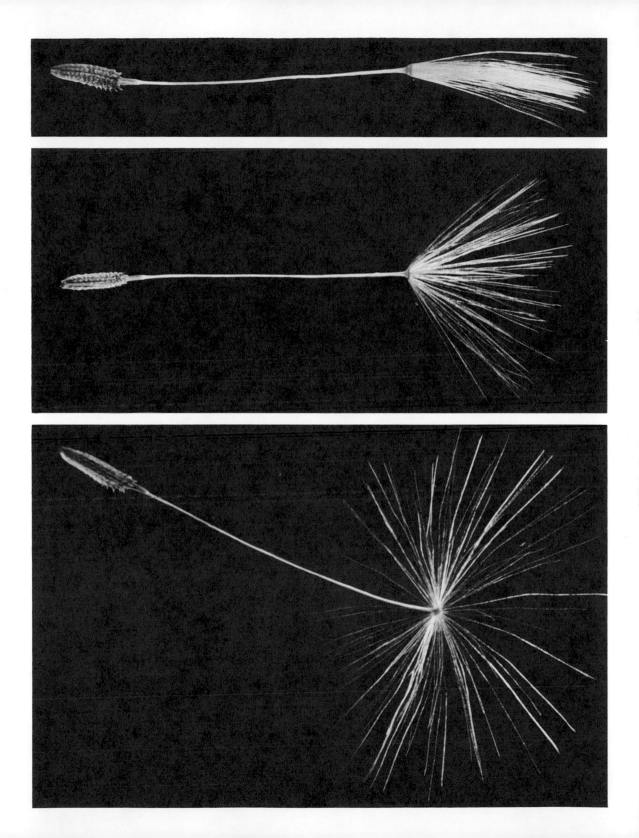

36 The length of the flower stem varies
depending on where it grows.
In a lawn regularly clipped by a lawn mower
the stem may be no more than three inches long.
But a dandelion growing in tall weeds
may rise two feet or more,
enabling its seeds to be scattered by the wind.

See if you can find
dandelions with double flower heads.
Double flower heads
mean double the amount of seeds.

38   The dandelion is a pest to people who like neat lawns.
Some of them crawl on hands and knees for hours,
digging up dandelions.
Often they throw the plants into a corner of the backyard.
There, even though uprooted,
the dandelion flower heads go through their entire cycle
and produce seeds that fly into the air
and produce lots more dandelion plants.

The dandelion is hard to get rid of
for another reason.
Its tap root goes down about a foot into the ground.
Only a portion of the root
of the plant in this photograph has been dug out,
yet it measures over nine inches in length.
The dandelion plant can grow deeper into the ground
than other lawn plants.
It finds moisture there that the other plants cannot reach.
The length of the root also protects it
from nibbling rabbits, moles, and insects.

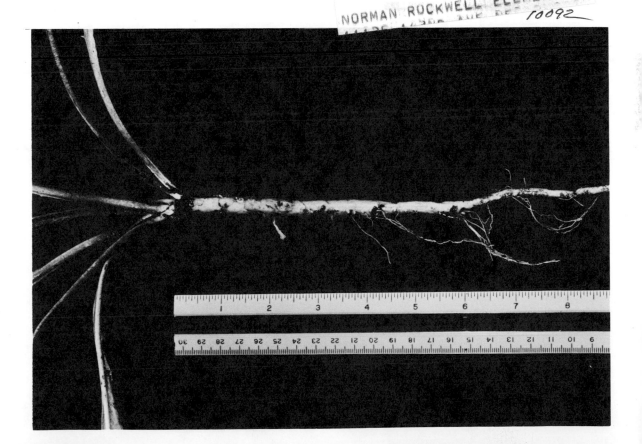

40   The dandelion is a perennial,
which means it lives on from year to year.
The top leaves and flowers die,
but the root lives on underground.
As it grows it divides,
and so the plant spreads.
The root shown here has divided,
and each branch has produced several plants.

The tap root also may get big enough
to support many plants instead of just one.

All these adaptations
help to make the dandelion an extremely hardy plant
and a difficult weed to control.

42   But dandelions have their uses.

The white fleshy root of the dandelion
is a food for some people.
They scrape the roots, slice them,
and boil them in salt water like potatoes.
American Indians considered them a food
as well as a medicine.
Once the people who lived on the island of Minorca,
east of Spain,
remained alive by eating dandelions
after a swarm of locusts destroyed
all other green plants on the island.

Dandelion roots can also be cleaned, baked,
ground up, and used as a coffee substitute
or mixed with regular coffee.

Young dandelion leaves
are considered a tasty vegetable by many people.
The leaves of plants
that have not yet flowered in the spring
are mixed with other greens in salads.
The leaves from older plants are not used
as they become tough and bitter.

Seed houses have been developing dandelions
with better-tasting leaves
than those of the wild dandelion.
The leaf on the top was grown from a seed-house seed.
The one on the bottom was grown from a wild seed.
Which is likely to be tenderer and sweeter?

44 Dandelion leaves are rich in vitamins A and B
as well as in calcium, phosphorous, and iron.
All these vitamins are present
if the leaves are eaten raw.
Dandelion leaves can be cooked too—like spinach.
Then they lose some of their vitamin value,
but they are still a healthful food
because of the minerals in them.

Besides being useful,
dandelions are fun to play with.
You can blow on the blowballs,
whistle through their stems,
make dandelion-flower necklaces,
and slit the stems so that they curl.

46 Now we know why fields and lawns
become quickly covered with dandelions.

Millicent E. Selsam's career has been closely connected with biology and botany. She majored in biology and was graduated *magna cum laude* with a B.A. degree from Brooklyn College. At Columbia she received her M.A. in the Department of Botany, and since then she has passed all course requirements and a comprehensive examination for a Ph. D., also at Columbia. After teaching biology for ten years in the New York City high schools, she has devoted herself to writing science books for children.

Mrs. Selsam lives in New York City and spends her summers on Fire Island, New York.

Jerome Wexler was born in New York City, where he attended Pratt Institute. Later he studied at the University of Connecticut. His interest in photography started when he was in the ninth grade. After service in World War II, he worked for the State Department in Europe as a photographer. Returning to the United States, he specialized in photographing advanced farming techniques, and the pictures he made have been published throughout the world.

Now chief photographer for *Visual Teaching,* an audiovisual company specializing in slide sets and filmstrips for use in schools, Mr. Wexler lives in Wallingford, Connecticut.